The B-24J, Delectable Doris.

RADIO COMPASS

LEGEND
Power
Radio Compass
Marker Beacon
Flex Cable

Page 186] RADIO COMPASS EQUIPMENT

Chapter V
RADIO COMPASS EQUIPMENT

RADIO COMPASS EQUIPMENT [Page 187

MACHINE CALIBER .50, M2, AIRCI

PIECE NO.	DESCRIPTION	PIECE N
B8916	PAWL—BELT HOLDING	B9718
B8925	LOCK—BREECH	B9731
B8928	LATCH—COVER	B9741
B8931	SPRING—SWITCH	B9632
B8943	SPRING—COVER LATCH	B17169
B8944	BAR—TRIGGER	B17171
B8946	EXTENSION—FIRING PIN	B147461
B8949	LATCH—BACK PLATE	B147463
B8951	SHIM—TRUNNION BLOCK	B147464
B8961	PAWL ASSEMBLY—BELT FEED	B147583
B8962	PIN ASSEMBLY—BELT FEED PAWL	B261110
B8963	PIN ASSEMBLY—BELT HOLDING PAWL	BFAX1BB
B8964	SHAFT ASSEMBLY—OIL BUFFER PISTON	BFAX1BB
B8969	VALVE ASSEMBLY—COVER LATCH	BFAX1BE
B8975	PAWL—CARTRIDGE ALIGNING	BFAX1BE

5

Designed by Dan Patterson. Edited by Melissa E. Barranco, Claudia J. Garthwait, and Ross A. Howell, Jr.

Library of Congress Catalog Card Number 93-79037

ISBN 0-943231-61-2

Printed and bound in Hong Kong.

Published by Howell Press, Inc., 1147 River Road, Suite 2, Charlottesville, VA 22901, telephone 804-977-4006.

First printing

HOWELL PRESS

Previous page : A collection of personal equipment from the crews of B-24s. At left are items of survival gear, a parachute pack and harness, the yellow "Mae West" life jacket, a fleece-lined flight helmet, oxygen mask and fleece-lined boots, so important at the 50-degree-below-zero temperatures at combat altitude. The playing cards carried aircraft spotting information.

This book is dedicated to Lt. Paul Gleason, and all the other young men who flew off to war in B-24s.

Preface

While I was growing up and reading all about World War II aviation (or so I thought), the B-24 was always "that other bomber." I fell victim to the lack of available history about this airplane. The B-24 had not received the same press and publicity bestowed on the B-17.

The B-24 was a military tool, a "Soldier." This airplane started as a superior performer to the B-17, flying faster and farther. The realities of aerial combat, particularly over Europe, dictated more guns carried in powered turrets, greater armor protection for the crew, and a heavier bomb load. Late model B-24s of the European Theater of Operations (ETO), when fully combat ready, couldn't fly as high or any further than the B-17. The B-24 had changed.

What did not change was the courage of the men who flew these bombers into enemy skies. The B-24 was an assemblage of metal, Plexiglas, wood, wire, and rubber that was used by these men to do their job. It was the crews that brought these airplanes to life. There would be no remembrance of these bombers without the crews who flew them into combat and came back with stories of their survival and the stories of their friends who did not return.

Dan Patterson
November 16, 1993

THE SOLDIER

Consolidated B-24 Liberator

Photographs by Dan Patterson
Text by Paul Perkins and Michelle Crean
with additional material by Joseph A. Ventolo, Jr.

The Soldier

The story of the B-24 Liberator began in January 1939 — when Chief of the Army Air Corps, General H. H. Arnold, decided that a second source of supply for four-engine bombers was needed. At that time, the Boeing B-17 was the only four-engine, long-range heavy bomber the United States possessed. Initially, Consolidated Aircraft Corporation was approached as a potential second producer for the B-17.

Less than two years before, a near destitute inventor, David R. Davis, had

thereby saving fuel that would otherwise be burned to overcome airfoil drag.

The Consolidated Model 31, later produced for the United States Navy (USN) as the P4Y-1 flying boat, was designed around the new Davis wing. This design took to the air in May 1939, and bested the top speed of the comparably sized PBY-3 Catalina by eighty miles per hour — and 1,000 miles in range.

On January 30, 1939, I.M. Laddon and David Fleet (son of Consolidated's president, Reuben Fleet) arrived at Wright

identical letters were sent to the Glenn L. Martin Company and Sikorsky Aviation Corporation enclosing Type Specification C-212 and Amendment No.1, dated December 16, 1938. Neither company had a design along the lines of AAC Type Specification C-212. On March 4, 1939, Authority for Purchase Number 147928 was initiated to cover procurement for the Model 32 (AAC designation XB-24).

The Model 32 bomber was almost entirely designed on the basis of tests carried out with the Model 31 flying boat.

The Consolidated Model 32(XB-24).

sold Consolidated his design for a high-performance airfoil. Initial wind tunnel testing results were so astounding that the technicians thought the tunnel was somehow malfunctioning. Airfoil efficiency was 102 percent—two percent greater than theoretically possible! The Davis wing developed high lift at low angles of attack,

Field with a model specification and preliminary data outlining a proposed heavy bombardment airplane to answer the 1938 Army Air Corps Type Specification C-212. This required a 300 MPH top speed, 3,000 mile range, 35,000 foot service ceiling, and a maximum payload of 8,000 pounds of bombs. On February 1, 1939,

For ease of ground maneuvering and in recognition of the Davis wing aerodynamics, the XB-24 employed tricycle landing gear (including a steerable nosewheel). The wing, borrowed directly from the Model 31, also featured Fowler flaps. These effectively increased the wing area to provide more lift, allowing slower landing speeds. The Davis wing promised, and delivered, longer ranges and heavier bomb loads than those of the B-17. Wing area was 1,048 square feet as compared to 1,420 square feet on the B-17. This meant a higher wing loading — which would translate into higher landing speeds. The XB-24 directly borrowed the twin-finned tail assembly of the Model 31. Engines on the prototype were Pratt & Whitney R-1830-33 Wasps of 1,000 horsepower at 14,500 feet and 1,200 horsepower on take-off. Consolidated expected a top speed

dered 38 additional B-24As on August 10, 1939.

Consolidated and Vultee Aircraft, Incorporated, merged in March 1943. A production history of the Liberator, supplied by Consolidated Vultee Aircraft Corporation in 1946, states that the XB-24 (Air Corps SN 39-556) made its seventeen-minute maiden flight on January 2, 1940. Most other sources give December 29, 1939, for the first flight. With a gross weight of 41,000 pounds, it carried .30-caliber guns in the nose (2), and waist

retained by Consolidated for further modification and testing, later to emerge under a new designation and serial number.

The original XB-24 prototype was accepted by the Army in August 1940. By then, it had become the XB-24B (Air Corps SN 39-680), with self-sealing fuel tanks and new turbosupercharged Pratt & Whitney R-1830-41 engines in redesigned oval cowlings which would characterize all subsequent Liberators. Intakes on each side supplied air to the supercharger and intercooler. Top speed increased from 273 to 310 MPH. This airplane was test flown well into 1944, after which Consolidated converted it to an executive transport. It served with the Army Air Forces until April 1946.

Meanwhile, France had placed orders for 175 aircraft. The designation was LB-30, which signified the thirtieth design proposal in Consolidated's Land Bomber series. This LB-30 designation was used for export versions up to the B-24D. France was overrun by the Germans so quickly that none of these was delivered. The Royal Air Force, desperate for aircraft, took over the contract (though reducing the number ordered to 139). Thus, most of the initial production B-24s, all manufactured by Consolidated's San Diego plant (the only B-24 assembly line at this point), went to England. Attempts to track Liberator production and disposition in the early years of WWII give one a sense of the gravity of the Allied position. The aircraft went wherever the immediate need was perceived.

As the design for the aircraft was developed, the gross weight of the XB-24 was increased by 5,300 pounds to 46,300 pounds. The XB-24 design appeared so promising and the AAF need for a second heavy four-engine bomber so great, that seven YB-24 aircraft were ordered before the prototype B-24 was completed. Only one of these seven aircraft ordered went to the United States. The other six, built in

B-24Js over a European target.

USAFM

with this installation of 311 MPH at 15,000 feet.

A mock-up inspection was completed on April 11, 1939. A service test order for seven YB-24 aircraft was placed on April 27, 1939. The projected performance looked so good, and the situation in Europe so bad, that the government or-

positions (2) and one in the dorsal and ventral positions. The open tail position was covered by a single .50-caliber weapon. Army flight testing commenced on February 10, 1940. Top speed was 273 MPH at 16,000 feet with a service ceiling of 27,000 feet. This performance fell short of Air Corps specifications, so the XB-24 was

December 1940 and serialed AM-258 to AM-263, went to Great Britain designated as LB-30As. They lacked self-sealing fuel tanks and spent their careers flying the North Atlantic route with Ferry Command.

The sole American YB-24 service test aircraft had to wait while a twenty-plane batch of LB-30Bs for the RAF was built. Finally, the YB-24 was assigned to the Army Air Corps Ferry Command Training School.

Twenty B-24A Liberator Is, initially intended for the Army Air Corps, were diverted to the RAF. These were built March to May 1941 and serialed AM-910 to AM-929.

One LB-30B (AM-927) never made it to British service. It was damaged in a landing accident in Albuquerque, New Mexico, July 24, 1941. The plane was rebuilt in the U.S. as a Consolidated executive transport. Today, it flies at airshows with the Confederate Air Force.

Three LB-30Bs went directly to British Overseas Airways Corporation as transports.

The remainder of the Liberator Is went to Number 120 Squadron RAF in Northern Ireland for antisubmarine duty. These aircraft were modified at Prestwick, Scotland, by the addition of Air to Surface Vessel Radar (ASV), depth charge racks in the bomb bays, and a forward-pointing quadruple 20mm cannon pack mounted just aft of the nose landing gear.

Liberator crews on antisubmarine patrol spent long hours of search punctuated by an occasional sighting of a periscope wake or surfaced submarine. Once in contact, the aircraft would maneuver into position, then fly low to bracket the submarine's conning tower with special bombs or depth charges. Hopefully, water pressure would crush the U-boat's hull. Typically, a submarine would rather escape attack by submerging, but if caught on the surface, it was capable of putting up defensive fire. Damaged aircraft were hundreds of miles from home — the merciless sea below. Air-sea rescue was well organized and frequently effective, but it was difficult to spot a single raft in a vast expanse of water — providing, of course, anyone escaped a ditched B-24.

The elegant roller shutter bomb bay doors, designed to reduce drag on bomb runs, tended to collapse on impact with the water. In 1942, provision was made for the bombardier to install bomb door stiffeners prior to ditching — thus reinforcing them and affording the crew more time to escape. In some cases, these curved "ditching ribs," two for each of the bomb doors, were fitted into brackets built into the underside of the center catwalk

A formation of B-24s from the 392nd Bomb Group.

USAFM

12

8th Air Force B-24s over Ploesti.

and the inside lip of the bomb bay door. In other cases, wooden stiffeners appear simply to have been wedged into place.

First enemy contact by British-operated Liberators was a German Fw 200 maritime patrol bomber which was driven away from a convoy on October 4, 1941. The Liberators, flying patrols of up to sixteen hours, covered the mid-Atlantic gap, sinking a total of eight U-boats during the war. One aircraft, AM-929, was a five-submarine "ace."

The nine B-24As that went to the United States Army Air Forces were built June to July 1941. (The U.S. Army Air Corps was redesignated the U.S. Army Air Forces, or USAAF, on June 20, 1941). In American service, the .30-caliber guns were replaced with .50-caliber weapons; gross weight increased yet again to 53,600 pounds. Engines were Pratt & Whitney R-

1830-33s. Two of these aircraft were fitted with cameras and slated for reconnaissance missions over bases on the Japanese-mandated islands of Truk, Jaluit, and Ponape. One was destroyed at Hickam Field during the attack on Pearl Harbor on December 7, 1941. The other aircraft returned to Air Transport Command (ATC).

LB-30s (Liberator IIs) had extended noses and Pratt & Whitney R-1830-S3C4-G engines with Curtiss (instead of the usual Hamilton) propellers. All were fitted with self-sealing fuel tanks. The British armed them with .303-caliber machine guns. The bombardier had one gun in the nose along with a Sperry O-1 bomb sight. There were a pair of .303s at each waist station, and a final .303 provided for the rear bottom hatch near the tail.

The first LB-30 flown cost the life of Consolidated's chief test pilot William

Wheatley, when a loose part fouled an elevator column chain and the plane went down during its acceptance flight on June 2, 1941.

Immediately following the attack on Pearl Harbor, the Army Air Corps requisitioned seventy-five aircraft, retaining the LB-30 designation and the British serial numbers. Only forty-five ultimately saw service with the USAAC, six were wrecked early on, and the other twenty-three were eventually returned to the British. One LB-30 became Winston Churchill's personal transport.

Fifteen American LB-30s were sent to reinforce the 19th Bombardment Group in Java in January 1942. The first American Liberator action of the war took place when three LB-30s teamed up with a pair of B-17s on a strike against Japanese shipping and airfields from Singosari, a

Dutch military airfield in Java, on April 2, 1942. Japanese Zero fighters tore into the group right after they had dropped their bombs. One Liberator ditched while a second crash-landed on the way home.

Another seventeen LB-30s went to the 6th Bombardment Group to defend the Panama Canal. Three went to the 28th Composite Group in Alaska to attack Japanese shipping. Those that did not serve as bombers were converted to transports and served with Ferry Command over both the Pacific and Atlantic routes of supply.

American LB-30s were fitted with a Martin upper turret (two .50-caliber machine guns), twin .50-caliber machine guns (non-turreted) in the tail, and single weapons at the waist and rear lower hatch (tunnel) positions. The top turret on the LB-30 was perched just aft the trailing edge of the wing. One hundred thirty-nine LB-30s were manufactured.

The B-24C design embodied lessons learned in the European Theater of Operations (ETO). It had self-sealing fuel tanks, a twin .50-caliber Martin top turret sitting just behind the cockpit, and a Consolidated twin .50-caliber tail turret. There was one .50-caliber gun mounted in the nose and one in each of the two waist positions. Engines were Pratt & Whitney R-1830-41s with exhaust-driven turbosuperchargers. The gross weight was increased slightly to about 54,000 pounds. Ironically, no B-24C ever saw combat; all were used for crew training and test missions.

The B-24D was the first series to be produced for the United States armed forces on a large scale. Between the USAAF and the RAF, they appeared in every theater of operation. Originally, the British received them as direct purchases, later through the Lend Lease program.

Early in 1941, recognizing the pro-jected requirements for more Liberators, the Liberator Production Pool was created. Under Army management, Consolidated built a second B-24 production facility at Fort Worth, Texas. Douglas Aircraft Company, Incorporated, opened a third plant in Tulsa, Oklahoma, initially to produce Liberators from sub-assemblies supplied by Consolidated. The fourth builder, Ford Motor Company, began deliveries from its massive Willow Run plant near Ypsilanti, Michigan, in September 1942. The fifth builder, North American Aviation, Incorporated, had a production facility in Dallas, Texas, which began deliveries in March 1943.

The gross weight of the B-24D ultimately rose to 60,000 pounds with many armament changes made during its production run. Field and depot modifications increased defensive firepower. Altered D-models were the first B-24s with a nose turret. Previous B-24s officially

A tight formation of B-24s approaches an enemy coast.

listed a crew complement of seven; the B-24D carried a ten-man crew, reflecting the need for additional gunners. The internal bomb load was 8,800 pounds, with provisions being made on some models to carry one extra 2,000-pound bomb externally under each wing. Of course, all specifications noted are for the aircraft under "ideal conditions." During combat operations, bomb loads were occasionally traded for fuel to increase range.

The USAAF, recognizing the Liberator's long-range capability, originally intended to concentrate large numbers of B-24s in the Pacific. Early in 1942 the "Halvorsen Detachment" (also referred to as HALPRO), comprising twenty-three B-24Ds under the command of Colonel Harry Halvorsen, was assembled to make a raid on Tokyo from bases in China in case Jimmy Doolittle's B-25 raid on Tokyo failed. Ordered to Asia via the Atlantic, the Halvorsen Detachment made it no further than the Middle East. On June 12, 1942, a dozen of these B-24s flying out of an RAF airfield at Fayid, Egypt, attacked the oil refinery complex of Ploesti, Romania.

This was the first of many attacks on Ploesti, the main supplier of oil and gasoline to the German war machine. On August 1, 1943, unescorted B-24s would attack the complex again. Going in, *the losses were expected to be fifty percent.* Mechanical problems, lousy weather over Greece, a botched approach to the target, murderous anti-aircraft fire, and determined fighter resistance combined to claim 53 of the 164 aircraft dispatched.

In the ETO, large, tight bomber formations flying at high altitudes to avoid heavy ground fire were the norm. The "box" formation was the key to survival. It was intended to yield maximum interlocking defensive firepower, bomb saturation of the target, and to keep the high squadron from bombing the low squadron.

Unescorted raids on targets such as Schweinfurt and Regensburg revealed that box formations with interlocking fields of defensive fire were not enough to prevent crippling losses of men and machines. German fighter tactics evolved quickly. Enemy fighters singled out individual squadrons, hammering that particular box to degrade the defensive fire.

The XB-41, an attempt to counter the frontal attacks of German fighters, was a B-24D fitted with the nose of a B-17G, plus two dorsal Martin A-3 turrets (one that could be elevated), and double waist guns. The total defensive armament went from ten to fourteen .50-caliber weapons. A total of 12,420 rounds of ammunition was carried! The XB-41 was developed in parallel with the XB-40 (a B-17 variant). Unlike the XB-40s, the XB-41 never saw combat. Its service ceiling was 18,000 feet — suicidal over a defended target in occupied Europe.

44th Bomb Group Liberators, note smoke markers dropped by lead bombers. USAFM

The B-24E marked the addition of the Ford Motor Company production line at Willow Run, Michigan.

The XB-24F was a B-24D equipped with a hot air deicing system for the wings and tail surfaces. Hot air gathered from heat exchangers in the engine exhausts also supplied anti-icing for the windscreens, nose turret, and top turret.

The first twenty-five B-24Gs built by North American Aviation in Dallas, Texas, had the D-model "greenhouse" nose. Thereafter, production B-24G aircraft carried nose turrets. Concurrently, Consolidated's Fort Worth plant, Douglas, and Ford's Willow Run plant were turning out a similar variant dubbed the B-24H. All -Hs were produced with the nose turret carrying twin .50-caliber weapons to answer the head-on fighter attacks in the European and Mediterranean theaters. Around this time, the retractable Sperry ball turret, first tried on some -Ds and -Es, was incorporated as standard equipment to cover the blind underside of the bomber.

The B-24J was regarded as the definitive nose-turreted B-24. First manufactured at Fort Worth on September 23, 1943, the B-24J was the Liberator produced in the greatest numbers. Like its predecessors in most respects, it also utilized the Consolidated Motor Products hydraulically operated nose turret. Later -Js also incorporated the new C-1 autopilot, the M-series bombsight, a simplified fuel transfer system, and electronically controlled turbosuperchargers. A minor visible difference was that the -J's nosewheel door opened inward instead of outward. Later examples were fitted with the exhaust-heated deicing equipment developed on the XB-24F.

The B-24J's gross weight of 65,000 pounds — more than twelve tons heavier than the prototype XB-24 — translated into high control forces and sluggish response. To shed some of this poundage and increase stability, -Js sent to the Southwest Pacific theater after September 1943 usually had the ball turrets removed at modification centers in the United States. With the increased availability of long-range escort fighters, the ball turrets were discarded in England early in 1944.

In January 1945, Lieutenant General James H. Doolittle, Eighth Air Force Commander, wrote Barney M. Giles, Chief of Air Staff, "... no minor modifications will make the B-24 a satisfactory airplane for this theater (ETO) of operations." Increasing the defensive firepower, which included a formidable nose turret, had combined with other modifications to substantially increase the weight, reduce the aerodynamic quality, and unacceptably reduce the overall utility of the aircraft. The load-carrying capacity of the B-24J was reduced to 5,000 pounds for long-range high-altitude operation.

Increased gasoline consumption and reduced speed cut the B-24's radius of action in the ETO. By contrast, lighter configured B-24s flying at lower altitudes in the Pacific excelled as long-range performers until the arrival of the B-29 Superfortress.

Account of Ed Redden, Eighth Air Force, 446th Bomb Group, 706 Lead Crew, Copilot, B-24J, Hot Shot Charlie.

"Mid-January 1945, the formation had formed up at 21,000 feet and crossed the northern French coast. Flak hit engine number four. We lost control of the prop governor which flipped Hot Shot Charlie on its back in the middle of the high right squadron. The nose went down, and the engine continued to run away, throwing us into a tight spin through the clouds."

Pilot Paul Armentrout and Ed Redden were standing on the rudders as every instrument red-lined.

"We were going straight down from 21,000 feet to 14,000 feet when the plane gradually responded enough to be pulled out of the spin.

"Paul hollered to Ed on the intercom, 'For God's sake! Don't pull it out too hard, the wings may come off!' An estimated seven or eight g forces were pulled before leveling off. We determined that we lost engines number one and two (on the same side), engine number four ran away, and number three developed carburetor ice and stopped.

"During the spin someone yelled to salvo the bombs, but no one could move, and then it became apparent we were upside down. No time to be salvoing a full bombload.

"Engine number three was restarted; engine number four was feathered. Then engines number one and two were restarted. Once the engines were restarted, we salvoed the bombload in the channel and were directed to a large RAF field in Scotland where we landed."

This was to be Hot Shot Charlie's last landing. Rivets in the wings were popped, the wing struts were torn; the plane was salvaged for parts and never flew again.

Doolittle felt perhaps the greatest handicap to bombing efficiency in the B-24 was tight quarters for the bombardier and navigator with the nose turret interfering with forward vision. Seventy-five percent of mission failures were caused by poor navigation. Inaccurate navigation through specified corridors substantially increased flak losses. To find and destroy small targets from high altitude, both the navigator and bombardier needed adequate forward vision.

The chin turret desired by Doolittle, which appeared on many modified B-24s, was a Bell power- boosted twin .50-caliber unit from the Martin B-26 tail emplacement. It was situated below the modified greenhouse nose common to B-24D variants. This turret improved the nose aerodynamics and gave the bombardier and navigator greater working room and a better forward view. However, there was a shortage of B-24D greenhouses to graft onto existing Liberators (some of which varied due to different manufacturers). Moreover, the scarce Bell units were usually provided to the Ninth Air Force (ETO) and their B-26 Marauders.

The B-24N promised to correct these aerodynamic and visibility deficiencies, but never made it into large-scale production or combat.

Military requirements for effective combat use of an aircraft differed widely between the two theaters. European operations were carried out in fairly close cooperation with the British, therefore radio, radar, and other equipment differed from those of aircraft operating in the Pacific theater. Missions in the South Pacific were flown over vast expanses of water, working with Navy installations at widely scattered shore stations. Radar equipment for the ETO permitted bombing of land targets from considerable altitude, while in the Pacific Theater of Operations (PTO), radar bombing was done from lower altitudes against tactical targets and shipping.

Engines #3 and #4, a formation of B-24s and the target. USAFM

The worldwide use of the B-24 necessitated the simultaneous requirement for in excess of fifty distinct types of modifications. Modifications were carried out at seven different centers with the prime contractor's assistance when possible. Modifications accomplished on a production line required a minimum of 500 to a maximum of 6,000 man-hours for some of the more complicated radar and photographic installations. On V-J Day the modification centers held more than four hundred B-24s in storage awaiting modifications prior to final delivery to the USAAF. Space previously devoted to B-24 modifications was taken over by the higher priority B-29 Superfortress.

There were other versions of the B-24 Liberator with later designations than "-J."

The XB-24K, built in January 1945,

and later redesignated XB-24N, was a Ford-modified B-24D with a ball-shaped nose turret and single fin and rudder. Stability, speed, and rate of climb performance were measurably improved, which led to an order for a B-24N variant. Events however, intervened, and of the more than five thousand ordered, only seven were produced by Ford through June 1945.

The B-24L variant attempted to correct the tail-heaviness of earlier Liberators. The tail turret was lightened by two hundred pounds. Ford and San Diego built 1,667 from July 1944 to January 1945. One B-24L became the XB-24Q, used as a test bed by General Electric to develop the radar-directed tail turret for the Boeing B-47 Stratojet.

When the last B-24 rolled off the line at Willow Run on June 29, 1945, production of all B-24 variants totaled 18,190 aircraft.

B-24 Little Warrior *hit by flak.* USAFM

The Air Crew

The combat air crew was a special group of men, welded by pride, skill, teamwork, and fighting spirit. Often the crew assembled stateside, trained together, shipped out together either by sea or in a brand-new airplane, and served together once overseas. They did not always stay together — the odds of completing a 25-mission combat tour in 1943 averaged around 35 percent. Crew changes occurred due to casualties, illnesses, mission requirements, and personality clashes — but once a crew was formed, its members tried to remain a team.

Pilot and Copilot

The pilot was the airplane commander; the B-24 and crew were his charges. He was responsible for the safety and efficiency of the crew at all times — not just when flying and fighting, but for the full twenty-four hours of every day he was in command.

How well each crew member contributed as a member of the combat team greatly depended on the command skill of the pilot. The pilot needed to know each member of the crew as an individual and take a personal interest in him. Like the commander of any force, large or small, he set the tone for morale.

Success as airplane commander was grounded in the respect, confidence, and trust the crew felt for him. This respect needed to be for him as an individual — not the position he held. He needed to understand his job and duty — and to convince the crew that he knew his stuff. The pilot needed to be friendly, understanding, but firm. He had to be fair and impartial in his decisions. The decision — once made — had to be final. Crew discipline bred comradeship and high morale as a natural byproduct.

The airplane commander was coach in a sport with mortal stakes.

The copilot was the pilot's execu-

Account of Kirby H. Woehst, Fifteenth Air Force, 454th Bomb Group, 738th Squadron, Flight engineer and top turret gunner, B-24H, Tail Wind.

"April 12, 1944. Another big raid way up into Austria proper. We were routed to fly right through the flak. We missed the flak, but the ME-110s, JU-88s, ME-109s and FW-190s jumped us right over the target. We got our ship shot up pretty badly. Most of the tail of our ship was shot up — but it got us home.

"May 22, 1944. Target was the harbor and marshaling yards at La Spezia, north of Rome. We hit a few bursts of flak and one of them cut our gas line to #3 engine. Gas poured into the bomb bays. There was a hole in the wing big enough to put your hand through. I slid down out of the turret and opened the door to the bomb bays. It was a sea of gasoline and fumes. Immediately upon discovery of all the loose gasoline, everything that was electrical was turned off...one spark and it would have been all over. The boys clear back in the tail of the ship were all drenched in gasoline. I cracked the bomb bay doors before we started any of the other procedures to get rid of the gas and the fumes. Tail Wind *again came home on three engines."*

tive officer, chief understudy, and strong right hand (both figuratively and literally). He had to be familiar with all the pilot's responsibilities and duties. Promotion, courtesy of fighters or AA, meant the copilot would have to fly the B-24 with the same skill as the pilot. Both pilots were instrument flight qualified — able to fly good formation in any assigned position, day or night. They had to be proficient at navigation, day or night, by pilotage, dead reckoning, or by radio aids (primarily the radio in the cockpit).

Copilots frequently went on to take over their own ships and crews with mixed emotions, proud to assume command — regretful at leaving the old team. Good pilots facilitated this transition by giving their copilots their fair share of flying responsibility.

Radio Operator

The radio operator had the least glamorous job in a B-24. His position was in the upper fuselage aft of the cockpit and top turret. This fellow sat for hours on end, static crackling in his ears, giving position reports every thirty minutes, assisting the navigator in taking fixes, and informing headquarters of targets attacked and results. Sending any distress signals was his responsibility. He maintained the equipment in good working order, maintained a log, preflighted the radio equipment, and frequently acted as the crew photographer. Finally, the radio operator was responsible for first-aid equipment he fervently hoped would stay unused.

Engineer

The engineer had to know more about the B-24 than any member of the crew — including the airplane commander. The lives of the entire crew, the safety of the equipment, and the success of a mission rested squarely on his shoulders. In emergencies, it was the engineer to whom the airplane commander turned.

Bombardier

Accurate and effective bombing was the ultimate purpose of the B-24 and crew. Every other function was preparatory to hitting the target. The bombardier's job required close cooperation with the pilot and a mutual understanding of their duties. During the brief interval (usually less than three minutes) of the bomb run

A 453rd Bomb Group B-24.   USAFM

— the bombardier was in absolute command. He told the airplane commander what was needed: until the bombs left the racks his word was law. The bombardier controlled the aircraft on the bomb run, either through the auto-pilot or Pilot Directional Indicator (PDI). The auto-pilot connected directly to the bombsight; the PDI transmitted desired course changes to the pilot via a needle instrument in the cockpit.

The bombing problem was a function of many variables.

1. *Altitude*, controlled by the pilot, determined the length of time the bombs were in flight and affected by atmospheric conditions. The forward travel of the bombs (range) and deflection (distance the bombs drifted in a crosswind with respect to the aircraft's ground track) were a function of time from release to impact. The altimeter needed to be calibrated and correct — and the pilot had to maintain the assigned altitude as accurately as possible. For every additional one hundred feet above the assumed bombing altitude of twenty thousand feet, bombing error increased by thirty feet.

2. *True airspeed*, controlled by the pilot, was the measure of the B-24's speed through the air. The true airspeed of the bomb determined the trail of the bomb —

A B-24 with engine #2 smoking . USAFM

the horizontal distance the bomb lagged behind the bomber at the moment of impact. Once the bombing airspeed and altitude were entered into the bombsight — they had to be maintained. For erroneous airspeed, bombing error increased approximately 170 feet for a 10 MPH change.

3. *Bomb ballistics* tables for each type of bomb described their intended trajectory from bomber to target.

4. *Trail,* mentioned earlier, was available from bombing tables and set in the bombsight by the bombardier. Trail was affected by altitude, airspeed, bomb ballistics, and air density — the first two factors being controlled by the pilot.

5. *Actual time of fall* was affected by altitude, type of bomb, and air density.

6. *Ground speed,* the speed of the B-24 in relation to the earth's surface, affected the range of the bomb and varied with airspeed, controlled by the pilot.

7. *Drift,* determined by the direction and velocity of the wind, was the distance the bomb traveled downwind from the aircraft on its journey to the target. Drift was set on the bombsight by the bombardier.

The best area bombing results were achieved by having a lead bombardier sight for the whole formation. The rest of the formation's bombardiers "toggled," released their bombs, precisely on the lead bombardier's drop or marker.

The "lead crew" concept was intended to improve both navigation and bombing accuracy. The cream of a group's navigators and bombardiers were assigned specific target areas for intensive study. After poring over aerial photos and sand table models and flying dozens of practice missions in ground trainers, each team could recognize its target from any altitude and direction. Thus, the choice of lead crew for a mission was based upon a crew's target of specialization, frequently with the mission commander as pilot, the regular pilot as copilot, and the copilot riding the tail gun position as observer.

Navigator

Navigation was a combination of dead reckoning (using speed and time elapsed between checkpoints to compute position), pilotage (watching the ground for visible landmarks), radio usage, and celestial navigation. The B-24 navigator had his own Plexiglas bubble just forward of the cockpit through which he could shoot his fixes. Celestial navigation was only used when delivering the aircraft to theater. In combat navigation, all bombing targets were approached by pilotage. The position accuracy expected was one-quarter mile. The limited outward visibility in Liberators with nose turrets made navigation by pilotage and dead reckoning a real headache. Frequently, the lead ship would substitute a navigator for the gunner in the nose turret — just to watch the ground.

Instrument calibration was an important duty of the navigator — since all navigation and bombing depended directly on the accuracy of his instruments. Correct calibration required close cooperation and extremely careful flying by the pilot. Instruments to be calibrated included the altimeter, compasses, airspeed indicator, astrocompass, astrograph, drift meter, and sextant.

Before the mission the pilot and navigator studied the route to be flown and selected alternate airfields. The pilot advised the navigator on weather expected, airspeed, and altitude that the mission was to be flown. Checkpoints were discussed. Once in the air, the pilot needed to fly consistent airspeed and course — and notify the navigator of any changes.

Gunners

The number of gunners on a B-24 varied with the mission and type of aircraft. All gunners necessarily were experts in aircraft identification, possessed a good sense of timing, and needed to know where to place their hits for maximum effect. With high rates of closure, evasive action, and the rolling and pitching of the bomber through turbulent air, it was difficult, if not impossible, to get a decent shot.

Waist gunners had the distinction of manning the position with the most casualties. It was the least well protected, and frostbite was a major concern.

Small men were generally chosen as ball turret gunners. There was no room for a parachute in this cramped position. The gunner kept the turret in constant rotation on lookout and to aim. He usually did not climb in until well after takeoff, and climbed out again before landing. From the standpoint of numbers and types of battle wounds, the ball turret was statistically the safest position. However, the lonely man in the ball turret of a B-24 was least likely to escape should catastrophe occur. The ball turret on B-24s could be retracted up into the fuselage to reduce drag when not in use.

In the ETO, missions meant routinely spending two to twelve hours in a shaking metal box, in subzero temperatures, with oxygen masks rubbing the skin off faces, and incessant engine noise making conversation impossible except by inter phone. The intense cold blasting in through open gun apertures and around the nose turret of later B-24s was somewhat countered by heaters and bulky electric flying suits. According to some reports, frostbite outnumbered all other combat injuries. Most crew members agreed that flak was far worse to endure than fighter attacks (though they would have preferred to encounter neither). They couldn't fight those thirty-yard-across black puffs blossoming all around them, nor sidestep the shrapnel that routinely ripped through the aluminum skin of the fuselage. There were almost no evasive maneuvers possible as fighters bore down upon them.

Delectable Doris

When the war ended, so ended the need for large weapon stockpiles. Armies were demobilized, and draftees "recycled" into civilian jobs. Some professional soldiers whose services were no longer needed by the Allies turned mercenary, working for whichever governments were willing to support them.

Designed and built for the sole purpose of delivering tons of bombs to a distant target, the Liberator did not prove to be especially adaptable to nonmilitary or peacetime roles. A world tired of war was not interested in preserving examples of weaponry for posterity. That concern would come later — too late for thousands of B-24s. Most were scrapped, their components sold, and their airframes melted down to reappear as pots, pans, and Chevrolets.

Delectable Doris, the airplane photographed for this book is fifty years old — a piece of living history. The aircraft has never been restored to perfection by any museum or group, and actually carries 1944-vintage equipment intact from its last operational assignment. About 90 percent of its operational equipment is aboard. Most of the walk-around oxygen bottles are still in place throughout the airplane. Web ration bags hang from their stations, cartridge chutes remain in the gun mounts, and extra .50-caliber ammo boxes are in place. The radio compass, three receivers, two transmitters, modulator, and inter phones are all at their assigned positions, though all but the last are non-operational. Fold-down tables, crew seats, and canvas curtains are present. Missing are a few portable oxygen bottles and the thermite self-destruct device once clipped to a bulkhead just aft of the bomb bay.

The B-24 Liberator, whose production run was greater than any other aircraft type manufactured by the United States in World War II, is represented by a mere handful of survivors. Only three are flying.

There is disagreement among those who flew it as to whether or not the Liberator was a good design. One fact seems apparent. The bottom line for many who loved the B-24 was, *"it kept bringing me back."*

Account of Melvin Oxsen, Fifteenth Air Force, 484th Bomb Group, 824th Squadron, Navigator and bombardier, B-24J.

"Our fuel transfer pumps were shot out; the engineer and the pilots discovered that they could transfer fuel by flying the bomber banked at a forty-five-degree angle and let gravity move the fuel. So we trimmed the plane to fly that way to transfer the fuel first from one side and then the other."

The usual altitude over a target for a B-24 was 20,000 feet.   USAFM

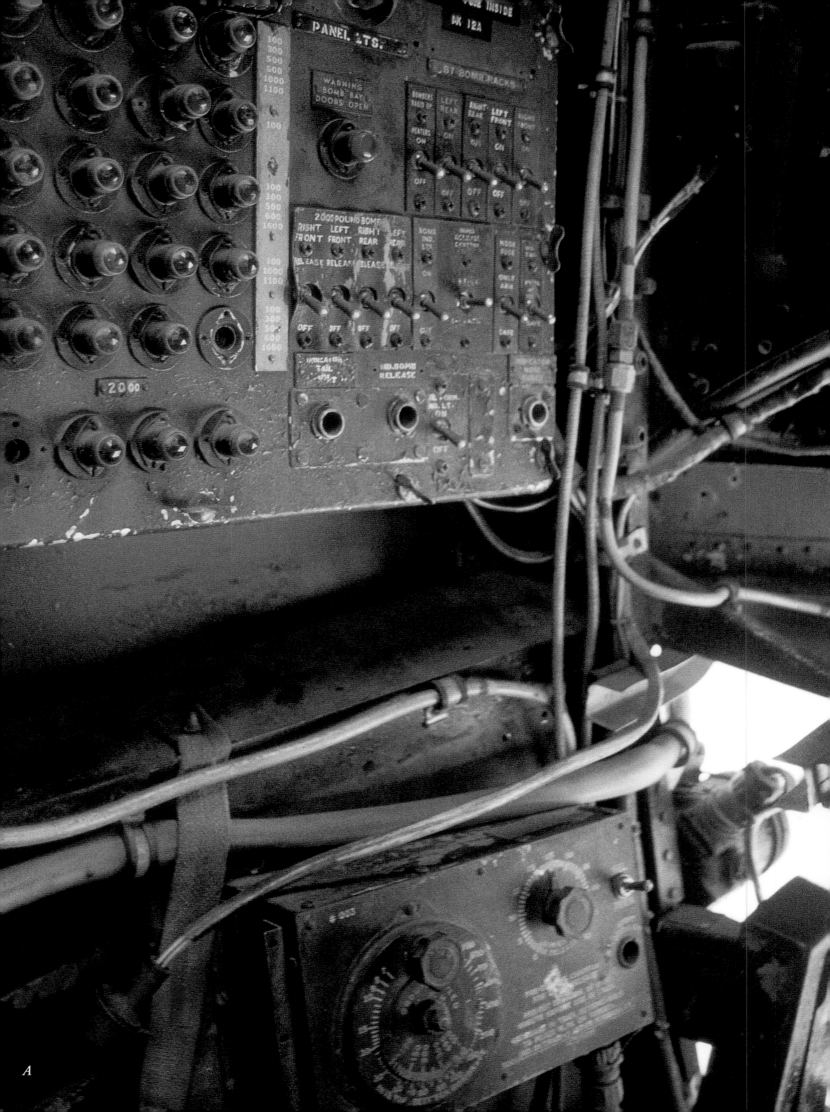

A

Previous pages:

A. This is the bombardier's view from behind his Mk 14 bombsight as he crawled forward under the nose turret to reach his station. Adding the power turret to defend the bomber against deadly frontal fighter attacks severely curtailed the forward vision of the bombardier.

B. The bombardier had to lie flat on his belly to bring his eye up to the bombsight. When the bomb run began, he put aside the distractions of flak outside and the nose turret above as it fired on attacking fighters. During the bomb run he controlled the bomber through his bombsight coupled with the autopilot, which made minor corrections to keep the airplane straight and level.

A. To the bombardier's left was the control panel that informed him of the status of the bombs. Below the panel was the intervalometer which controlled the timing of bomb release. The bombs could be released in a salvo (all bombs dropped at once), or timed to be "walked" across the target.

B. Engine #4 viewed from the nose through the right side window.

C. The drift meter at the top was an instrument to gauge the amount of lateral drift across an aircraft's ground track. Below was the track to carry .50-caliber ammunition to the nose turret.

D. Just aft of the control panel were the hydraulic controls for the bomb bay doors.

(In above and subsequent diagrams, gray area denotes aircraft section depicted in photographs.)

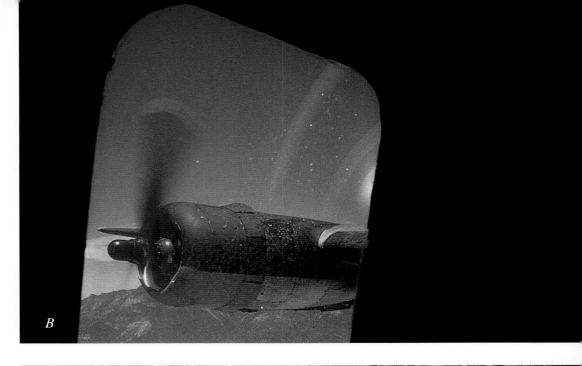

B

C

D

A

A. Directly above the bombsight was the powered nose turret. The gunner in this position was literally sitting on the nose of the bomber. This cylinder of Plexiglas and steel was electrically powered; the gunner pointed himself at the oncoming fighters. The B-24 Liberators were not pressurized. As they flew through the upper atmosphere, a subzero, 150+ MPH slipstream found its way around the turret into the fuselage.

If the crewmen in the nose had to bail out, they made their way out of cramped positions and crawled aft along the nosewheel to drop out through the opened nosewheel doors.

B. The nose turret gunner had to be constantly alert for enemy fighters.

C. Looking towards the twelve o'clock position through the gunsight.

Cockpit of the B-24J. The main instrument cluster was in the center of the panel. Also in the center was the panel that controlled the autopilot. On the center pedestal were the engine controls (left to right): turbocharger control, throttle levers, and fuel mixture controls. Below these levers were toggle switches to control propeller RPM, cowl flap positions, and the intercoolers. In front of the copilot's seat were the instruments that monitored engine performance. The red buttons on top of the panel were switches to destroy secret parts of the bomber if a forced landing was made in enemy territory. Above the magnetic compass were the propeller feathering controls. These turned the propeller blades of a stopped engine knife-edge to the relative wind, thereby reducing drag.

A

A. The pilot and copilot in the "front office" of the B-24. Light pouring through the greenhouse canopy made the cockpit appear more spacious than it was. The pilot was the airplane commander and responsible for the military well-being of his crew. The copilot was his executive officer. During long missions the ordeal of high-altitude formation flight was shared by these men.

B. After the preflight inspections were complete and the checklists were done, the pilot would signal to the ground crew below that he was ready to start engines.

C. Lt. Stan Staples, 461st Bomb Group, remembered that "we used to synchronize the props by leaning our heads back so that we could watch the shadow pattern of the blades. If the shadow moved toward or away from you, the engines were not on the same RPM, but when the shadow stood still, the RPM were synchronized and the engines would purr."

Collection of F. Bradley Peyton III

The top turret gunner, perched inside a Plexiglas bubble atop the bomber, had to keep alert for fighters that could attack from all points of the sky.

USAFM

A

A. *Looking to the six o'clock position from the top turret. The Martin-built turret had automatic firing stops to prevent the gunner from shooting off the tail of the bomber, something that could easily occur in the chaos of aerial combat.*

B. *The top turret gunner was also the flight engineer, here looking towards the three o'clock position to monitor the engines and watch for fighters. Engines #3 and #4 and the right wing.*

A

A. The duties of the flight engineer were to assist the pilot and copilot in monitoring the performance of the engines and to keep track of fuel burn. During combat missions fuel had to be transferred from one tank to another, particularly if battle damage had occurred. Fuel needed to be conserved. The sight gauges at the top right were part of the monitoring system. Beyond the bulkhead was the bomb bay; above was the center wing section that held the fuel tanks and plumbing necessary to keep the engines running. The red handle ran the emergency system to lower the main landing gear.

B. The flight engineer's electrical panel monitored the generators.

C. The top turret gunner/flight engineer was the senior enlisted man of the crew.

D. While the mechanical components of the turret were made of steel and Plexiglas, the interior sections were wooden, much like the staves of a barrel.

C

PATENTS REG. U.S. PAT. OFF.

GUN TURRET ASSEMBLY

TYPE 250 CE15   SERIAL NO.

ORDER NO. WRD 053 67   SPEC. NO.

DWG. NO. 250 CE150   VOLTAGE

THE GLENN L. MARTIN COMPA

U.S.A.

D

A

A. In earlier models of the B-24, the navigator's position was in the nose with the bombardier. When later versions added the nose turret, the area became crowded, and field modifications were made to move the navigator behind the pilot and the radio operator further aft. The navigator's duty was to maintain situational awareness, which meant knowing where the bomber was at all times, informing the pilot of upcoming course changes, and knowing how to plot a course home if it became necessary to leave the formation.

B. Engine #2 seen through the side window over the navigator's table.

A

A. Bomb bay of the B-24. At the top is the center wing section that the fuselage was built around. Tubing visible is part of the fuel transfer system. Beyond the bulkhead in the waist section are the yellow bottles of oxygen for the crew at high altitudes. The large beams running vertically are supports for the bomb racks.

B. Bomb doors on the B-24 rolled up the side of the fuselage. Hydraulically operated, the doors created much less drag than those that opened into the slipstream. During long missions the doors were opened slightly to ventilate the bomber. B-24s could accumulate dangerous levels of flammable vapors, which sometimes resulted in an airplane exploding in a fireball.

C. One of the electrical connections that held a bomb in place until released on command from the bombardier.

Next page: A crewman traverses the narrow catwalk that is the only path between the front and back of the bomber. This passageway was narrow when on the ground — in flight, for a crewman wearing full flight gear while the bomber was being tossed about by flak and formation turbulence — it was treacherous. The green bottle is a "walk-around bottle" that provided a few minutes of breathing oxygen for use while moving about the bomber. These bottles could be refilled at an oxygen outlet near any crew station.

41

B

C

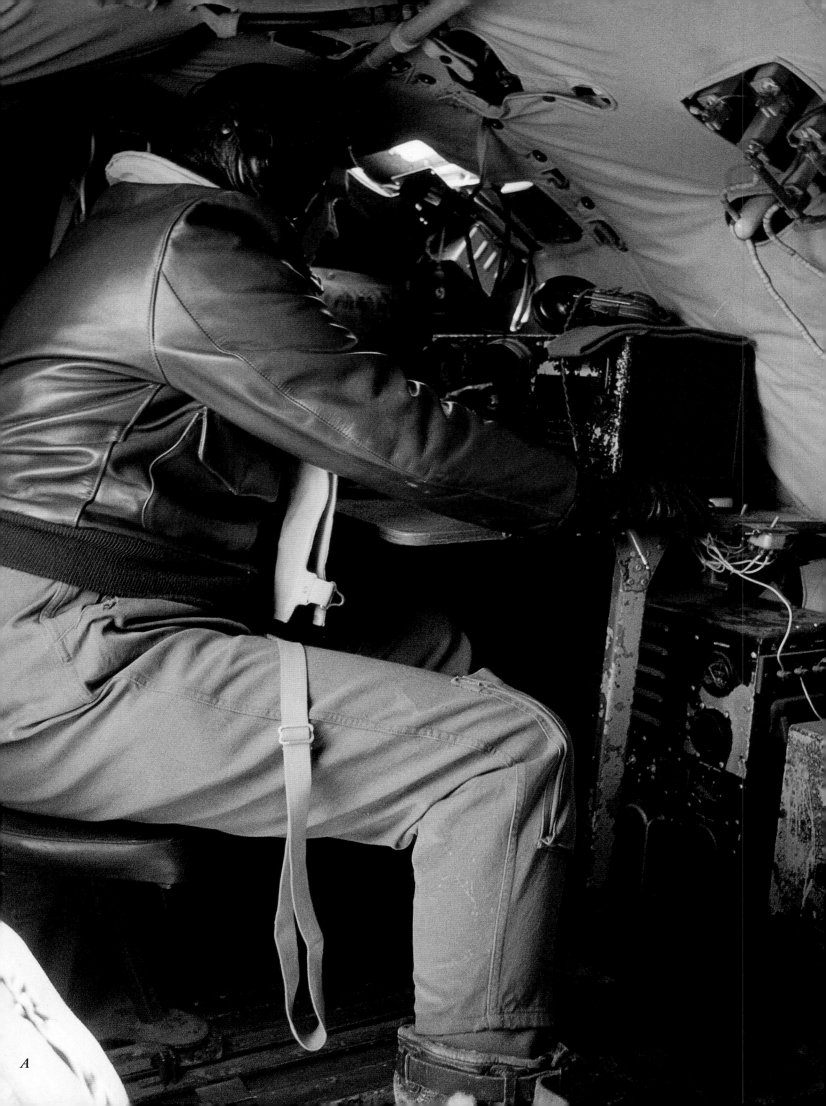

A

B

Previous page: Above the bomb bay (seen through hatch at bottom), the radio operator's position.

A. *The duties of the radio operator were to maintain contact with the commander of the formation by monitoring command channels and transmitting position reports every thirty minutes based on information given to him by the navigator. Radio operators also were expected to be proficient gunners in case they were needed to replace a wounded crewmate.*

B. *The work table of the radio operator.*

C. *U.S. Army Air Forces bombers carried trailing low-frequency antennas that were unspooled behind the airplane to receive transmissions from their bases. This control box told the operator how much of the antenna had been reeled out.*

45

C

A

A. Looking forward from the waist area, a crewman makes the long reach to climb from the bomb bay into the rear section of the bomber. To his right are the well and hoist for the ball turret. In this bomber the turret was replaced with an airborne radar unit. This unit as well as the ball turret were retractable and were deployed only when needed during a mission. Above the hoist are oxygen bottles, along the side of the fuselage are canvas clips and bags to hold flares, first-aid kits, and walk-around bottles. At top right is a hose that connects the crewman with the bomber's oxygen system. The red handle below opened a wind deflector that partially directed the 150 MPH slipstream away from the open waist windows.

B. Looking towards the ten o'clock position from the left waist window. Engine #1 and the left wing are visible. The waist gunner's duties included informing the pilot of any visible problems with the engines.

C. The crewman's view as he entered the bomber through the main entry hatch under the fuselage aft of the waist area. The waist windows opened upwards and latched into place to allow freedom of movement.

USAFM

47

B

C

A

A. The waist gunners had to swing their 65-pound, .50-caliber machine guns against the slipstream while tracking enemy fighters. These men, back to back, sometimes bumping into each other and often slipping on empty shell casings, had to remember not to shoot off parts of their own airplane.

B. Before every mission these men loaded their weapons onto the bomber. Forward of the open window is the retractable wind deflector.

Collection of F. Bradley Peyton III

B

A. Looking to the eight o'clock position from the right waist window. The distinctive vertical stabilizer of the B-24 is visible.

B. A small window under the horizontal stabilizer looked out to the rudder. At left is an empty holder for another walk-around oxygen bottle. Above the window is a light for interior illumination, across the window is part of the controls that, by a series of direct mechanical connections and cables, gave the pilot directional control of the bomber.

C. Left vertical stabilizer.

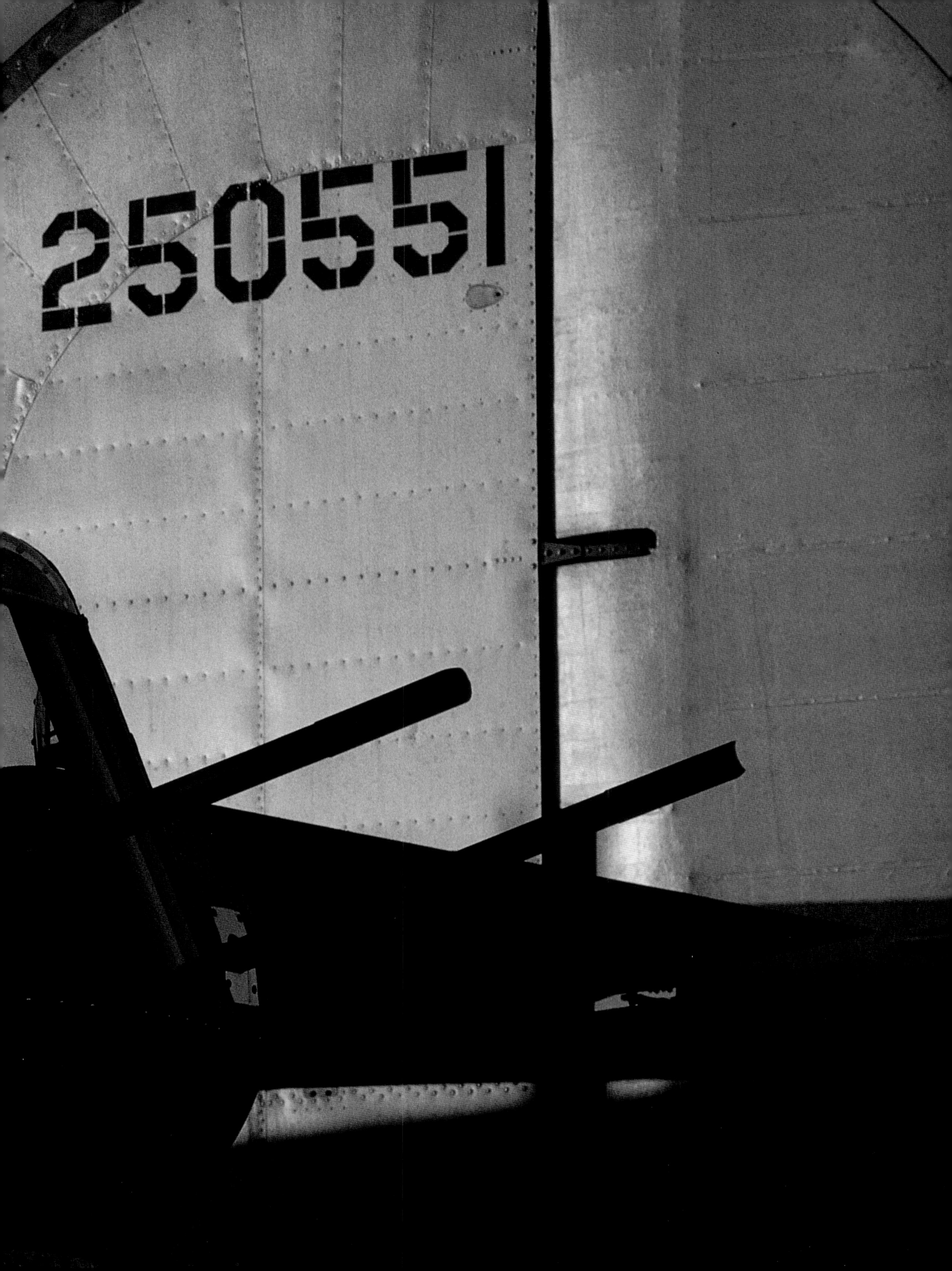
25055I

Previous page: Protecting the tail was the powered turret with two .50-caliber machine guns. Crewmen often painted names on their positions, either their own name, or the name of a girlfriend, wife, or mother.

A. Tail gunner in his position.

B. Looking towards the six o'clock position from the tail turret, the tail gunner had an unrestricted and often spectacular view of the following formations, the results of aerial combat, or the bombs that had just been dropped.

C. The tail turret was placed with what seemed a liberal tolerance of clearance between the turret and the fuselage. The gunner stepped into the turret and sat down, the gunsight directly in his vision. The "T" handle controlled the rotation of the turret and the elevation of the guns. The unit was operated by a hydraulic system totally independent of the bomber's main hydraulic system.

This model of the B-24 was powered by four Pratt & Whitney Twin Wasp R-1830-43, 14-cylinder, twin-row radial engines. The engines were rated to develop 1,200 horsepower on takeoff, and were turbosupercharged to furnish compressed air to the fuel induction system at sea level pressure while flying at high altitude. These engines were so reliable that a crew chief said it was "like having a DC-3 on each wing." The three-bladed propellers were Hamilton Standard, hydromatic full-feathering, constant speed. Each propeller weighed 500 pounds.

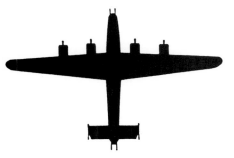

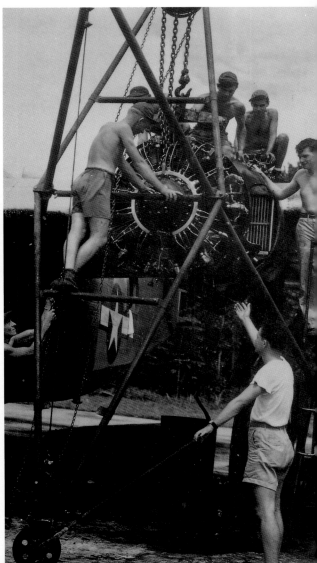

A

A.   The high wing placement and deep fuselage of the B-24 necessitated tall main landing gear. The struts and wheels retracted   into the wing between the inboard and outboard engines. At the top right is the turbosupercharger for engine #4. The bomb bay doors are open.

The main landing gear lowered on the downwind leg of the landing approach. The waist gunners reported to the pilot when the main gear were down and locked.

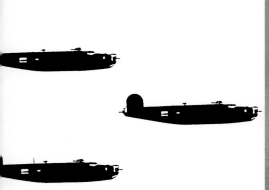

59

A

A. *Ground crews worked in all types of weather to keep the numerous and complex systems in working order. One cannon shell ripping through the maze of control cables, electrical connections, and hydraulic plumbing could create countless hours of repair and maintenance work.*

B. *The ground echelon worked on the airplanes up to the time of engine start. They topped off fuel tanks and polished the Plexiglas, removing any smudge that could hide an oncoming fighter. From some bases fuel requirements for a mission were so extreme that after the bombers had taxied out to the runway, their fuel tanks were topped off again just before takeoff.*

A. *After crew briefings, specialists on the crew often had a separate briefing to cover their area of expertise. While waiting at the bomber to climb aboard, these men would discuss the briefings with their crewmates.*

B. *Sometimes the complex schedules were thrown awry by bad weather, either at the base or over the proposed target. This made waiting or "sweating" out a start time a regular part of the bomber crew's life.*

C. *When it was time to go, the crewmen, dressed in their flight gear, went to war.*

Collection of F. Bradley Peyton III

USAFM

Acknowledgments

Virtually all the photographs taken for this book were done in David Tallichet's B-24, *Delectable Doris*. His help and participation made this book possible. This B-24 is unique in that it has not been restored; the airplane is truly a window into the past. Mr. Tallichet flies his airplanes "GI" (government issue), as they were operated during World War II. The paint is not perfect, the interiors have the look of use and wear, a perfect photographic setting to get a feel for the experiences of the crews who actually flew these bombers.

Rosann, my wife, for her support and understanding when I go chase airplanes. Nate, Brigitta, and Joe, our kids, who get to see "Dad" act like a kid too.

Ross Howell and Howell Press for continuing belief and support as this series continues.

With special thanks to F. Bradley Peyton III for sharing his memories and personal materials from his experience as pilot of *Tail Wind*, a B-24H Liberator of the 738th Squadron, 454th Bombardment Group (Heavy), Fifteenth Army Air Force. Peyton flew thirty-eight combat missions, thirteen of which were double-credit missions. He was awarded the Distinguished Flying Cross with Cluster, the Air Medal with seven Oak Leaf Clusters, and the President's Distinguished Unit Citation (twice). Other members of *Tail Wind*'s crew were William M. Giesa, copilot; Alfred O. Lee Jr., navigator; Gerald W. Lambert, bombardier; Kirby H. Woehst, engineer and top turret gunner; James C. Fisher, tail gunner; George M. Foote, ball turret gunner; Herbert W. Gray, nose gunner; Warren E. Hearne, waist gunner; Armine W. Lewis, tail gunner; Shirley Strother, radio operator and waist gunner.

The United States Air Force Museum and its Director, Colonel Richard Uppstrom, USAF(Ret) for access to the reference library and the B-24D, *Strawberry Bitch*, that resides in the museum. Joe Ventolo, Jr., Curator, Bob Spaulding, Dick Tobias, Dave Mennard, Nick Apple, and Wes Henry.

I would also like to thank Ed Redden, John Hess, Jeff Ethell, Air Vice Marshal Ron Dick, RAF(Ret), and Melvin Oxsen.

Technical Notes

The original photography in this book was all done with the intent to as faithfully as possible remove the clues of the present day and try to look back through a window opened by the owners and operators of these aircraft, a window into the 1940s when formations of these airplanes flew over the European continent during World War II.

I used a variety of cameras and equipment to complete this project: a Wista 4x5 Field View camera, with a 150mm Caltar II lens and a 90mm Nikkor lens; a Mamiya RB67 with 50mm, 90mm, and 180mm lenses; and a Nikon F3 with a motor drive and a garden variety of Nikkor lenses.

All the photographs were shot as transparencies to make the best possible color separations.

The 4x5 and 6x7 photos were all shot on Kodak Ektachrome Daylight film. The 35mm photos were all taken with Kodachrome 200.

The concept, design, and the photographs are done by Dan Patterson, 6825 Peters Pike, Dayton, Ohio 45414.

The Association of Living History, comprising the crewmen in these photographs, is an organization that is dedicated to the preservation and remembrance of the aircrews of the Second World War. The association provides historically accurate crewmen and women for airshows featuring the aircraft of World War II. Each member carefully researches the background, uniform, and crew positions to create a realistic impression of the soldiers who flew and fought in the airplanes of the 1940s.

Their input and technical advice were invaluable as this project evolved.

Bombardiers	Robert Clyborn and Tom Horton
Navigator	Natalio Banchero
Pilot	Glenn Sherwood
Copilot	Rob Barnes
Top Turret	John Wilson
Radio	Craig Smith
Ball Turret	Eric Steinman
Waist	Roger Condron
Tail	Barry Hildebrandt

Additional Crewman	Ron Shelby

Bibliography

BOOKS:

AAF: Official World War II Guide to the Army Air Forces. New York: Bonanza Books, 1988.

Andrade, John M. *U. S. Military Aircraft Designations and Serials Since 1909.* England: Midland Counties Publications (Aerophile) Ltd., 1979.

Birdsall, Steve. *The B-24 Liberator.* New York: Arco Publishing Company, Inc., 1968.

_____. *The B-24 Liberator,* Blue Ridge Summit, Pennsylvania: Aero Division of TAB Books, Inc., 1968.

Blue, Allan G. *The B-24 Liberator: A Pictorial History.* New York: Charles Scribner's Sons, 1975.

Bowman, Martin. *The B-24 Liberator: 1939-1945.* Chicago, Illinois: Rand McNally & Company, 1980.

Comer, John. *Combat Crew.* New York: Pocket Books, 1989.

Davis, Larry. *B-24 Liberator in Action.* Carrollton, Texas: Squadron/Signal Publications, Inc., 1987.

Dorr, Robert F. *U. S. Bombers of World War II.* London: Arms & Armour Press, 1989.

Freeman, Roger A. *B-24 Liberator at War.* New York: Charles Scribner's Sons, 1977.

_____. "The Consolidated B-24J Liberator." *Aircraft in Profile, Vol. 1, Part 2.* Leatherhead, Surrey, England: Profile Publications Limited, 1965.

Heflin, Woodford Agee, ed. *United States Air Force Dictionary.* Washington, D.C.: Air University Press, 1956.

Higham, Robin, and Carol Williams, ed. *Flying Combat Aircraft of the USAAF-USAF, Vol. 2.* Ames, Iowa: Iowa State University Press, 1978.

Jones, L. S. *U.S. Bombers, B-1 to B-70.* Los Angeles, California: Aero Publishing, Inc., 1962.

Spick, Mike. *Fighter Pilot Tactics.* Cambridge, England: Patrick Stephens Ltd., 1983.

Sunderman, Col. James F., ed. *World War II In the Air: Pacific.* New York: Van Nostrand Reinhold Company, 1981.

Swanborough, Gordon and Peter M. Bowers. *United States Military Aircraft Since 1909.* Washington, D.C.: Smithsonian Institution Press, 1989.

Thetford, Owen. *Aircraft of the Royal Air Force 1918-1958.* London: Putnam & Co., Ltd., 1958.

Wagner, Ray, *Liberator: 50th Anniversary B-24 Special Edition.* San Diego: San Diego Aerospace Museum, 1989.

Watry, Charles A. and Duane L. Hall. *Aerial Gunners: The Unknown Aces of World War II.* Carlsbad, California: California Aero Press, 1986.

Wegg, John. *General Dynamics Aircraft and Their Predecessors.* Annapolis, Maryland: Naval Institute Press, 1990.

DOCUMENTS:

"B-24 Serial Number 40-702." U. S. Air Force Museum Research Division, A1/(Y)B-24/his.

"Eighth Air Force B-24 Modifications." 8th AF/AAF Evaluation Board, ETO.

"Index of Serial Numbers Assigned to Aircraft Through Fiscal Year 1958," Procurement Division, USAF Air Material Command, Wright-Patterson AFB, Ohio.

"Pilot Training Manual for the Liberator B-24." Headquarters, AAF, Office of Flying Safety, 1944.

"Production History of the B-24 Liberator." San Diego, California: Consolidated Vultee Aircraft Corporation, January 1946.

"XB-24 (XB-24B) Serial Number 39-680 (39-556)," U. S. Air Force Museum Research Divsion, A1/(X)B-24/his.

PERIODICALS:

DeGroat, Robert S. "Geneseo '88." *Warbirds,* November/December 1989.

Dorr, Robert F. "B-24 Liberator: The Mostest." *Air Power History,* Spring 1990.

Eaker, Ira C. "The Flying Fortress and the Liberator." *Aerospace Historian,* June 1979.

Jacobsen, Meyers K. "Third Liberator En Route to U. S. From India." *AAHS Journal,* Winter 1973.

Jonsen, Frederick A. "Liberator Lore." *Air Museum Journal,* 1989.

Oughton, James D. "Do You Want to Buy A Liberator?" *Aviation News,* Vol. 2, No. 11.

Smith, Gene. "Flying the Mighty Liberator." *Warbirds International,* September/October 1989.

Vernonico, Nick. "Liberator." *Flypast,* December 1989.

Dan Patterson is a self-employed photographer, graphic designer and private pilot living in Dayton, Ohio. Previous books are *Shoo Shoo Baby, A Lucky Lady of the Sky* and *The Lady: Boeing B-17 Flying Fortress.*

Paul Perkins is an emergency room physician living in Yellow Springs, Ohio. His first book was *The Lady.*